No Bad Parts

THE WORKBOOK

Copyright © 2023 by GuideGuru Publishing

All rights reserved. No part of this publication may be reproduced, distributed, or transmitted in any form or by any means, including photocopying, recording, or other electronic or mechanical methods, without the prior written permission of the publisher, except in the case of brief quotations embodied in critical reviews and certain other noncommercial uses permitted by copyright law. For permission requests, write to the publisher at the address below.

Disclaimer:

This workbook provides general information on trauma, the Internal Family Systems Model, and related concepts. It is not a substitute for professional advice or therapy. Individual experiences may vary, and seeking personalized support from qualified professionals is recommended. By using this workbook, you agree to the terms outlined in this disclaimer. If you have any questions or concerns, consult with a qualified mental health professional or healthcare provider.

Thank you for choosing to engage with this book. We hope it helps you build a healthy and loving relationship with your partner.

LESSONS IN THIS WORKBOOK:

1. Understanding Trauma and Its Effects

2. The Internal Family Systems Model: An Overview

3. Accessing the Inner Landscape

4. Healing Exiled Parts

5. Working with Protective Parts

6. Transforming Traumatic Legacies

7. Living from the Self: Wholeness and Integration

Chapter 1: Understanding Trauma and Its Effects

Lesson 1:

Trauma can result from various experiences and can have a profound impact on an individual's psyche and functioning.

Think about a specific traumatic experience from your past and reflect on how it has impacted your life. Write down:
- What was the traumatic event or experience?
- How has it influenced your thoughts, emotions, or behaviors?
- In what ways has it affected your relationships or daily functioning?

Consider the different aspects of your life (e.g., childhood, relationships, work) and identify any potential sources of trauma. Write down:
- What are some events or experiences that might have been traumatic for you?
- How do you currently cope with the effects of those traumatic experiences?
- Are there any areas where you feel particularly stuck or affected by trauma?

_____
_____
_____
_____
_____
_____
_____
_____
_____
_____
_____
_____
_____
_____
_____
_____
_____
_____
_____
_____

Imagine a future version of yourself who has healed from their traumatic experiences. Reflect on the changes you would like to see in your psyche and functioning. Write down:
- What would it look like to be free from the impact of trauma?
- How would your thoughts, emotions, and behaviors be different?
- What steps can you take to move towards that future version of yourself?

Lesson 2:

Trauma often leads to the fragmentation of the self, where different parts of the personality emerge to protect the wounded core.

Identify and name some of the protective parts of yourself that have emerged due to past traumas. Write down: What are some parts of yourself that you recognize as protective? What roles or functions do these parts serve? How do these protective parts impact your day-to-day life?

Reflect on how the fragmentation of your self has affected your overall well-being and sense of identity. Write down: In what ways do you feel disconnected or fragmented within yourself? How does this fragmentation impact your relationships or ability to pursue your goals? Are there any areas where you would like to experience more wholeness and integration?

Imagine having a compassionate conversation with one of your protective parts. Write a letter to that part, expressing gratitude for its efforts and exploring its intentions. Write down: What part would you like to connect with and understand better? What do you appreciate about this part and its role in your life? How can you work together with this part to create more harmony and integration within yourself?

Lesson 3:

Internal Family Systems Model provides a framework for understanding and addressing trauma by acknowledging the existence of different parts within an individual's internal system.

Draw a diagram or write a list of the different parts within your internal system. Explore their characteristics and roles. Write down:
- What are some of the distinct parts you can identify within yourself?
- How would you describe the characteristics or qualities of each part?
- How do these parts interact or influence each other?

Reflect on how the Internal Family Systems Model can be applied to your own healing journey. Write down:
- How does the idea of different parts within yourself resonate with your own experiences?
- In what ways can acknowledging and understanding these parts help in your healing process?
- Are there any specific challenges or questions you have about applying this model to your own life?

Imagine engaging in an internal dialogue with one of your parts using the Internal Family Systems Model. Write a conversation between yourself and that part. Write down:
- What specific part would you like to connect with and understand better?
- How does this part typically express itself or communicate with you?
- As your compassionate Self, how would you approach and interact with this part to foster healing and integration?

_____
_____
_____
_____
_____
_____
_____
_____
_____
_____
_____
_____
_____
_____
_____
_____
_____
_____
_____
_____
_____
_____

Chapter 2:
The Internal Family Systems Model: An Overview

Lesson 1:

The Internal Family Systems Model views the mind as a system consisting of different parts, each with its own desires, emotions, and functions.

Reflect on different aspects of your personality and identify specific desires, emotions, or functions associated with each aspect.
Write down:
- What are some aspects of your personality that you can identify?
- What desires or goals are associated with each aspect?
- How do these aspects contribute to your overall functioning and well-being?

Choose one specific aspect of your personality and explore its desires, emotions, and functions in more detail. Write a journal entry:
- Describe this aspect and its characteristics.
- What desires or needs does it have?
- How does it express itself or influence your thoughts, emotions, or behaviors?

Imagine having a conversation with one of your parts, giving it a voice to express its desires, emotions, and functions.
Write a dialogue:
- Choose a part that you would like to explore more deeply.
- Start a conversation with that part, allowing it to share its desires, emotions, and functions.
- Reflect on how this conversation helps you understand and connect with that part on a deeper level.

Lesson 2:

The model identifies three types of parts: exiles, managers, and firefighters, each serving distinct protective roles within the internal system.

Reflect on your own internal system and identify instances where you recognize the presence of exiles, managers, or firefighters.
Write down:
- Can you identify any parts that may serve as exiles, managers, or firefighters within you?
- What are the roles or functions of these parts in your internal system?
- How do they manifest in your thoughts, emotions, or behaviors?

_____
_____
_____
_____
_____
_____
_____
_____
_____
_____
_____
_____
_____
_____
_____
_____
_____
_____
_____
_____
_____
_____
_____
_____

Choose one specific part (exile, manager, or firefighter) and explore its protective role in your life. Write a letter to that part:
- Address the part and acknowledge its presence and importance in your internal system.
- Express gratitude for the protection it has provided.
- Reflect on how this part has impacted your life and discuss any challenges or concerns you may have regarding its role.

Imagine having a compassionate conversation with a part that serves as a manager or firefighter. Write a dialogue:
- Choose a part that you perceive as a manager or firefighter and want to understand better.
- Start a conversation with that part, expressing curiosity and compassion.
- Explore its intentions, fears, and the strategies it employs to protect you.

Lesson 3:

The goal of IFS therapy is to help individuals develop a harmonious relationship between their parts and access their core Self, which is naturally calm, compassionate, and curious.

Reflect on your current relationship with your parts and your core Self. Write down:
- How would you describe your relationship with your parts?
- Do you feel connected to your core Self? If not, what barriers or challenges do you encounter?
- What would it look like to have a more harmonious relationship with your parts and a stronger connection to your core Self?

_____
_____
_____
_____
_____
_____
_____
_____
_____
_____
_____
_____
_____
_____
_____
_____
_____
_____
_____
_____
_____
_____
_____
_____

Imagine connecting with your core Self and describing its qualities and characteristics. Write a visualization exercise:
- Close your eyes and imagine connecting with your core Self.
- How does it feel to be in the presence of your core Self? What emotions or sensations arise?
- Describe the qualities of your core Self (e.g., calmness, compassion, curiosity) and how it interacts with your parts.

Reflect on practical ways to cultivate a stronger connection with your core Self and develop a harmonious relationship with your parts. Write down:
- What are some activities or practices that can help you connect with your core Self (e.g., meditation, journaling)?
- How can you invite your parts to express themselves while maintaining a compassionate and curious stance?
- What steps can you take to integrate the qualities of your core Self into your daily life and interactions with others?

Chapter 3: Accessing the Inner Landscape

Lesson 1:

Developing a curiosity about one's internal experience is crucial for accessing the different parts within the internal system.

Take a few moments to sit in a quiet space and tune into your internal experience. Write down:
- What thoughts, emotions, or sensations are present in this moment?
- Can you identify any specific parts that might be active within you?
- How does it feel to approach your internal experience with curiosity and openness?

Choose one aspect of your internal experience that you often ignore or dismiss. Write a letter to that aspect:
- Address the aspect and acknowledge its presence.
- Express curiosity about its role or function within your internal system.
- Ask questions and explore its perspective, allowing for a deeper understanding of its existence.

Create a list of questions to guide your exploration of your internal experience. Write down:
- What aspects of yourself or your inner landscape would you like to understand better?
- Brainstorm a list of questions to ask yourself about these aspects.
- Use these questions as prompts for journaling or self-reflection to deepen your understanding and curiosity.

Lesson 2:

Mindfulness and self-compassion practices can facilitate the exploration of the inner landscape and the identification of different parts.

Engage in a mindfulness practice focusing on your internal experience. Write down:
- Choose a mindfulness technique (e.g., body scan, breath awareness) to practice.
- As you engage in the practice, observe your internal experience with non-judgmental awareness.
- Write about any specific parts or patterns that arise during the practice and how they make themselves known to you.

Write a self-compassionate letter to yourself, acknowledging the challenges and struggles you may encounter during the exploration of your inner landscape:
- Begin the letter with words of understanding and kindness towards yourself.
- Validate any difficulties or resistance you may face while engaging with different parts.
- Offer words of encouragement and self-compassion as you navigate your inner landscape.

Create a daily self-compassion ritual to support your exploration of the inner landscape. Write down:
- Identify a self-compassion practice that resonates with you (e.g., self-compassionate affirmations, self-compassionate touch).
- Establish a daily routine to engage in this practice.
- Reflect on the impact of the self-compassion ritual on your ability to approach your inner landscape with kindness and acceptance.

Lesson 3:

By becoming aware of the roles and functions of each part, individuals can gain insights into their protective mechanisms and their underlying vulnerabilities.

Choose one part of yourself that you would like to explore in more depth. Write a journal entry:
- Describe the role and function of this part within your internal system.
- Reflect on how this part has protected you in the past and the positive intentions behind its actions.
- Explore any vulnerabilities or underlying emotions associated with this part.

Create a visual representation of your internal system, mapping out the roles and functions of each part. Write down:
- Draw a diagram or write a list of the different parts within your internal system.
- Describe the roles and functions of each part.
- Reflect on the interplay and dynamics between these parts.

Write a letter of gratitude to each part within your internal system, acknowledging their contributions and expressing appreciation:
- Address each part individually and thank them for their roles and functions.
- Reflect on how their protective mechanisms have served you in various situations.
- Express gratitude for their efforts and their willingness to collaborate as you work towards integration and wholeness.

_____
_____
_____
_____
_____
_____
_____
_____
_____
_____
_____
_____
_____
_____
_____
_____
_____
_____
_____
_____
_____
_____
_____
_____
_____

Chapter 4:
Healing Exiled Parts

Lesson 1:

Exiles are the wounded parts of the self that carry the burden of traumatic experiences.

Reflect on a specific traumatic experience from your past and identify the exiled parts associated with it. Write down:
- What are the exiled parts that emerged as a result of this traumatic experience?
- How have these parts been affected by the trauma?
- How do these exiles manifest in your thoughts, emotions, or behaviors?

Choose one exiled part that you would like to explore and understand better. Write a journal entry:
- Describe the characteristics and qualities of this exiled part.
- Reflect on how this part has been affected by the trauma and the burdens it carries.
- Explore any memories, emotions, or beliefs associated with this exiled part.

Imagine having a compassionate conversation with one of your exiled parts. Write a letter to that part:
- Address the exiled part and acknowledge its pain and suffering.
- Express empathy and understanding for what it has been through.
- Explore how you can provide support and create a safe space for this exiled part to heal.

Lesson 2:

Healing exiled parts involves developing a compassionate and non-judgmental relationship with them, acknowledging their pain, and providing the necessary support.

Write a self-compassionate letter to yourself, acknowledging the pain and struggles associated with your exiled parts:
- Begin the letter with words of kindness and understanding towards yourself.
- Validate the pain and difficulties that your exiled parts carry.
- Offer words of compassion and support, reassuring yourself that you are committed to their healing.

_____
_____
_____
_____
_____
_____
_____
_____
_____
_____
_____
_____
_____
_____
_____
_____
_____
_____
_____
_____
_____
_____
_____
_____
_____

Create a list of self-care practices that can provide support and nurturing for your exiled parts. Write down:
- Identify self-care activities that you find comforting, soothing, or healing.
- Consider activities such as journaling, meditation, spending time in nature, or engaging in creative outlets.
- Commit to integrating these self-care practices into your routine as a way to support your exiled parts.

Write a gratitude letter to one of your exiled parts, expressing appreciation for its resilience and strength:
- Address the exiled part and acknowledge its courage in carrying the burden of the trauma.
- Express gratitude for its protective efforts and the strengths it has developed.
- Reflect on how you can collaborate with this exiled part in its healing journey.

Lesson 3:

By working with exiles, individuals can release the emotional burdens associated with trauma, leading to greater integration and wholeness.

Reflect on the emotional burdens associated with your exiled parts and how they impact your daily life. Write down:
- Identify the emotions and burdens that your exiled parts carry.
- Reflect on how these emotional burdens affect your thoughts, relationships, or behaviors.
- Imagine the freedom and relief that would come from releasing these emotional burdens.

_____
_____
_____
_____
_____
_____
_____
_____
_____
_____
_____
_____
_____
_____
_____
_____
_____
_____
_____
_____
_____
_____
_____
_____
_____
_____

Write a letter of release to one of your exiled parts, expressing your intention to let go of the emotional burdens associated with it:
- Address the exiled part and acknowledge the pain it carries.
- Affirm your commitment to healing and releasing the emotional burdens associated with it.
- Reflect on what it would feel like to experience a sense of lightness and liberation once these burdens are released.

Imagine engaging in a symbolic ritual to release the emotional burdens of your exiled parts. Write a description of the ritual:
- Describe the ritual, whether it involves writing, burning, or another form of symbolic release.
- Visualize yourself participating in the ritual, letting go of the emotional burdens associated with your exiled parts.
- Reflect on the sense of freedom and integration that comes from releasing these burdens.

_____
_____
_____
_____
_____
_____
_____
_____
_____
_____
_____
_____
_____
_____
_____
_____
_____
_____
_____
_____
_____
_____
_____
_____
_____

Chapter 5:
Working with Protective Parts

Lesson 1:

Managers and firefighters are protective parts that emerge to shield the individual from further harm and manage the internal system.

Identify and describe one of your protective manager parts. Write a journal entry:
- What is the role and function of this manager part within your internal system?
- How does it manifest in your thoughts, emotions, or behaviors?
- Reflect on times when this part has protected you or influenced your decision-making.

_____
_____
_____
_____
_____
_____
_____
_____
_____
_____
_____
_____
_____
_____
_____
_____
_____
_____
_____
_____
_____
_____
_____
_____
_____
_____
_____

Reflect on a specific situation where your firefighter part has emerged to protect you. Write down:
- Describe the triggering situation and the protective actions taken by the firefighter.
- Reflect on the intentions behind its actions and how it was trying to shield you from harm.
- Explore the positive aspects of this firefighter part's response and any potential challenges it may pose.

Choose one manager or firefighter part and personify it as a character. Write a short story or dialogue:
- Give the part a name and imagine its appearance, personality, and mannerisms.
- Create a story or dialogue where you interact with this protective part.
- Explore the dynamics between yourself and the part, acknowledging its protective role and discussing how you can work together more effectively.

_____
_____
_____
_____
_____
_____
_____
_____
_____
_____
_____
_____
_____
_____
_____
_____
_____
_____
_____
_____
_____

Lesson 2:

Understanding the intentions and fears of protective parts is essential for developing a cooperative relationship with them.

Write a letter to one of your protective parts, expressing your curiosity and willingness to understand its intentions and fears:
- Address the part and acknowledge its presence and importance in your internal system.
- Express a genuine desire to understand its intentions and fears.
- Ask open-ended questions, inviting the party to share its perspective and concerns.

Engage in a journaling exercise where you explore the underlying fears of a specific protective part. Write down:
- Choose a protective part and identify its primary fears.
- Reflect on how these fears have influenced its protective behaviors.
- Consider how these fears might be rooted in past experiences and traumas.

Write a dialogue between yourself and a protective part, where you discuss its intentions and fears. Write down:
- Start the dialogue by introducing your compassionate Self and inviting the protective part to share.
- Ask the part about its intentions and fears, and listen empathetically to its responses.
- Offer reassurance and understanding, exploring how you can address its fears while finding healthier ways to fulfill its positive intentions.

Lesson 3:

By acknowledging the positive intentions of protective parts and inviting them to collaborate, individuals can create a more balanced and harmonious internal system.

Reflect on the positive intentions behind the actions of one of your protective parts. Write a gratitude letter to that part:
- Express gratitude for the party's positive intentions and its efforts to protect you.
- Reflect on the ways in which this part has contributed to your well-being and safety.
- Discuss how you can work together more collaboratively to achieve balance and harmony within your internal system.

_____
_____
_____
_____
_____
_____
_____
_____
_____
_____
_____
_____
_____
_____
_____
_____
_____
_____
_____
_____
_____
_____
_____

Imagine engaging in a compassionate conversation with a protective part, expressing appreciation for its positive intentions.
Write a dialogue:
- Choose a protective part you would like to connect with and understand better.
- Start the conversation by acknowledging its positive intentions and the value it brings.
- Explore ways to collaborate with this part to find alternative strategies that align with your overall well-being.

Create a vision board or collage representing a balanced and harmonious internal system. Write a reflection on the visual representation:
- Gather images or words that represent balance, harmony, and collaboration.
- Assemble these images into a vision board or collage.
- Reflect on how this visual representation inspires you to acknowledge and integrate the positive intentions of your protective parts.

_____
_____
_____
_____
_____
_____
_____
_____
_____
_____
_____
_____
_____
_____
_____
_____
_____
_____
_____
_____
_____
_____
_____
_____
_____
_____
_____

Chapter 6: Transforming Traumatic Legacies

Lesson 1:

Traumatic legacies are patterns of behavior, beliefs, and emotions that persist beyond the initial traumatic experiences.

Identify and describe a specific pattern of behavior, belief, or emotion that you recognize as a traumatic legacy. Write down:
- What is the specific pattern or legacy that you want to transform?
- How does this pattern manifest in your life?
- Reflect on how this pattern may be connected to past traumatic experiences.

Write a letter to yourself, acknowledging the existence of the traumatic legacy and its impact on your life:
- Address yourself with compassion and understanding.
- Describe the specific behavior, belief, or emotion that you want to transform.
- Reflect on how this legacy has affected you and the areas of your life where you want to experience change.

Imagine your life without the influence of the traumatic legacy. Write a vision statement:
- Envision yourself free from the grip of the traumatic legacy.
- Describe how your behavior, beliefs, and emotions would be different.
- Reflect on the positive changes you would like to see in your life as you transform this legacy.

Lesson 2:

By identifying and understanding the origins of traumatic legacies, individuals can work towards transforming and releasing them.

Reflect on the possible origins of the traumatic legacy you identified earlier. Write down:
- Consider the specific traumatic experiences or events that may have contributed to this legacy.
- Reflect on the emotions, beliefs, or behaviors associated with those experiences.
- Explore any connections or patterns that you notice between the past trauma and the current legacy.

_____
_____
_____
_____
_____
_____
_____
_____
_____
_____
_____
_____
_____
_____
_____
_____
_____
_____
_____
_____
_____
_____
_____

Write a journal entry exploring the emotional impact of the traumatic legacy and its connection to the original trauma:
- Describe the emotions that arise when you think about the traumatic legacy.
- Reflect on how those emotions are linked to the original traumatic experiences.
- Consider any insights or realizations that come up as you explore this connection.

Imagine having a conversation with the younger version of yourself who experienced the trauma. Write a letter to that younger self:
- Address your younger self with compassion and empathy.
- Offer words of support and understanding for the pain they endured.
- Reflect on how you can provide the comfort, healing, and reassurance that your younger self needed during that traumatic time.

Lesson 3:

Through the integration of parts and the cultivation of self-leadership, individuals can break free from the grip of traumatic legacies and create new narratives for their lives.

Reflect on the different parts within your internal system that are influenced by the traumatic legacy. Write a list or draw a diagram:
- Identify the specific parts that are entangled in the legacy.
- Describe how these parts contribute to the perpetuation of the legacy.
- Consider how the integration of these parts can support the transformation of the legacy.

Write a letter to yourself as the Self, embodying the qualities of calmness, compassion, and curiosity:
- Address yourself from the perspective of the Self, the core essence within you.
- Express encouragement and guidance as you navigate the process of transforming the traumatic legacy.
- Reflect on the self-leadership qualities you can cultivate to support yourself in breaking free from the grip of the legacy.

Create a new narrative or affirmation that challenges the beliefs and behaviors associated with the traumatic legacy. Write down:
- Craft a statement or affirmation that represents the change you want to embody.
- Challenge the old beliefs and behaviors perpetuated by the legacy.
- Reflect on how this new narrative aligns with your values and aspirations for your life moving forward.

Chapter 7: Living from the Self: Wholeness and Integration

Lesson 1:

The Self represents the core essence of an individual, characterized by calmness, curiosity, and compassion.

Reflect on moments in your life when you have experienced a connection with your core self. Write down:
- Describe the characteristics of your core self, such as calmness, curiosity, and compassion.
- Recall specific moments when you have felt aligned with these qualities.
- Reflect on how it feels to embody the essence of your core Self and the impact it has on your well-being.

Write a letter to your core self, expressing your desire to cultivate a deeper relationship with it:
- Address your core self with respect and openness.
- Express your intentions and commitment to developing a connection with it.
- Reflect on how this relationship can enhance your sense of self and guide your actions and decisions.

Imagine engaging in a dialogue with your core self. Write a conversation between yourself and your core Self:
- Start the dialogue by introducing yourself and inviting the core self to speak.
- Ask questions to understand its wisdom, insights, and guidance.
- Reflect on the messages and guidance you receive from your core self and how you can apply it in your life.

Lesson 2:

By cultivating a relationship with yourself and integrating the different parts, individuals can experience a greater sense of wholeness and authenticity.

Identify a part of yourself that feels disconnected or in conflict with your core self. Write a journal entry:
- Describe the part and its characteristics, beliefs, or behaviors.
- Reflect on how this part feels separate from your core self.
- Explore ways to integrate this part and align it with your core Self to promote a greater sense of wholeness and authenticity.

Write a letter to a part of yourself that you want to integrate with your core self. Express your intentions for collaboration and harmony:
- Address the part with kindness and understanding.
- Acknowledge the positive qualities or intentions of the part.
- Share your desire to work together to achieve integration and alignment with your core self.

_____
_____
_____
_____
_____
_____
_____
_____
_____
_____
_____
_____
_____
_____
_____
_____
_____
_____
_____
_____
_____
_____
_____
_____
_____

Create a visualization exercise where you imagine embracing and integrating your different parts. Write a description of the visualization:
- Close your eyes and visualize yourself surrounded by your different parts.
- Envision embracing and integrating each part, feeling a sense of harmony and wholeness.
- Reflect on the emotions and sensations you experience during the visualization and the impact it has on your overall well-being.

Lesson 3:

Living from the self allows for more flexibility, creativity, and resilience in navigating life's challenges.

Reflect on a recent challenge or difficult situation you encountered. Write a journal entry:
- Describe the challenge and your initial response to it.
- Reflect on how you can approach the situation from a place of calmness, curiosity, and compassion rooted in your core self.
- Explore alternative perspectives or solutions that arise when you embody the qualities of your core Self.

Write a self-affirmation that reminds you to live from your core self in the face of challenges. Write down:
- Craft a statement that reflects your commitment to approach life's challenges with flexibility, creativity, and resilience.
- Use words that evoke the essence of your core Self, such as calmness, curiosity, and compassion.
- Repeat this affirmation to yourself regularly as a reminder of your intention to live from the Self.

Imagine yourself embodying the qualities of your core self in a challenging situation. Write a narrative of this scenario:
- Describe a specific situation where you encounter a challenge.
- Visualize yourself responding to the situation with flexibility, creativity, and resilience from your core self.
- Reflect on how this approach affects the outcome of the situation and your overall well-being.

Made in United States
Troutdale, OR
08/11/2023